VICIOUS SHARK ATTACKS

Why Sharks Attack And How To Stop Them

Bryan Coltrane

Copyright © 2017.

All rights reserved. No part of this publication may be reproduced, distributed, or transmitted in any form or by any means, including photocopying, recording, or other electronic or mechanical methods, without the prior written permission of the publisher, except in the case of brief quotations embodied in critical reviews and certain other noncommercial uses permitted by copyright law.

This book is intended for informational and entertainment purposes only. The publisher limits all liability arising from this work to the fullest extent of the law.

Table of Contents

Introduction

Sharks That Attack: 3 in 489

Shark Attack Sprees

The Great White Shark

The Tiger Shark

The Bull Shark

Shark Attack Prevention

Shark Attack Prevention by Country

Shark Attacks in the Media: News and Fiction

Introduction

With the popularity of movies like Jaws and the marketing success of the television programming known as Shark Week, sharks are on a lot of people's minds and shark attacks have become one of the most common fears.

The definition of a shark attack is a shark attacking a human. Despite this common fear that sharks are serial predators with a taste for human flesh, there are only around seventy shark attacks reported every year, across the globe.

The truth is shark attacks that fit some of our deepest fears are incredibly rare, like the attacks in 1916 at the Jersey Shore. There are

489 different species of sharks and only three of them have unprovoked, fatal attack reports that reach the double-digits; bull shark, tiger shark, and the great white shark.

Recorded statistics do not have information on castaways, so it is plausible that the whitetip shark that lives in the wide, open ocean may be responsible for unrecorded attacks as well.

Confirmed reports of unprovoked shark attacks from the year 1958-2014 show the United State (without Hawaii) has the most attacks total at 1104, with thirty-five of those being fatal attacks and the last fatality recorded was in 2012.

Australia has the second highest number of

shark attacks with 536 total, seventy-two of which were fatal and the last fatality recorded was in 2017.

Africa had a total of 346, with ninety-four of them being fatal and the last fatality in 2015. Asia had 129 total shark attacks, with forty-eight of them being fatal and the last fatality being in 2000. Hawaii on its own had 137 total shark attacks, with ten of them being fatal and the last fatality in 2015.

The Pacific Islands and Oceania (without Hawaii) had a total of 126 shark attacks with forty-nine of them being fatal and the last fatality in 2016. South America had a total of 117 with twenty-six of those being fatal and the last fatality in 2015. Antilles and the Bahamas had seventy total shark attacks with twenty-seven of those being fatal and the last fatality in 2013. The total number of shark attacks between those fifty-six years worldwide was 2,899 with 548 of those attacks being fatal and the last fatality being in 2017. That's an average of fifty-one shark attacks a year with only nine of them being fatal.

In yearly statistics, there were seventy-nine total reported shark attacks around the globe, with eleven of them being fatal. Those numbers lowered in 2005 and 2006 to sixty-one and sixty-two, with a total of four fatalities each year.

There were eighty-one total shark attacks in 2016, which matches the average for 2011-2015, which was eighty-two shark attacks a year. Out of those attacks, 58% of them were surfers. There were four total fatalities that year as well, with the average through 2011-2015 being eight. 2015 was the highest year on record for shark attacks, with ninety-eight total.

As the majority leader in total shark attacks, there are around sixteen attacks in the United States per year with one death in every two years, on average. The highest offenders for shark attacks are Hawaii, Florida, Texas, California, and the Carolinas and there has been at least one shark attack in almost every state along the coast.

The country with the highest number of deaths caused by sharks is Australia, and the deadliest place in the world when it comes to shark attacks is West Australia. Over the last forty years, both the total number of attacks and the number of shark-related deaths there has grown exponentially. There have been a total of sixteen deaths caused by sharks along the coastal areas in Western Australia since the year 2000. Divers there are now said to face a one in 16,000 chance that they'll suffer a fatal shark bite.

Other places with high shark attack reports include Boa Viagem in Brazil, Réunion Island, Maui, Makena Beach, Second Beach, Hawaii, South Africa, and Port St. Johns. Of those, one of the highest numbers of reported shark attacks comes from Africa, which has a death rate for shark attacks of 27%.

The singular location that has the highest number of reported attacks by sharks is New Smyrna Beach in Florida.

Though these recorded incidents are reported and have become statistics, there is no way to accurately count every single shark attack in the world. For instance, there is no way to consistently send out accurate shark attack reports from Third World countries along the coasts. They have more important things to concern themselves with than shark attack statistics, so the numbers reported are likely to be lower than the real totals.

Even so, they show that there is no real serial-attacking, mass-murdering sharks out there attacking every human in sight; and those that do attack unprovoked are rare. Nations that are developed like the United States and Australia provide more thorough shark attack reports than coastal nations that are still developing. The technological advancements in those two places especially have allowed them to take the lead in documenting shark attack data, which may be why they are also the highest totals; they may just be more accurate than the other nation's recordings. The International Shark Attack File is kept up by institutions and individuals in the US, South Africa, and Australia and devoted to keeping a regularly updated database on shark attacks.

It may seem as though these numbers are high, proving that shark attacks are something that anyone who visits the coast should be afraid of, but when compared to the statistics for other deaths by nature it's obvious how small the risk of shark attack is comparison. As an example, lightning strikes in coastal areas kill more than thirty-eight people on average per year, versus the average of less than one per year in Florida. If you only use the people that go to beaches in the United States in your ratio statistics, there is a one in 11.5 million chance of getting attacked by a shark and less than one in 264.1 million chance of being killed by one.

Sharks That Attack: 3 in 489

One of the biggest misconceptions about sharks is that they're all vicious, deadly creatures that are programmed by nature to attack everything. In reality, there are 486 different species of shark and there are only three of them that are known to be responsible for a number of unprovoked attacks that reaches two digits.

These three types of sharks are the bull shark, tiger shark, and the great white shark. However, there is a theory that the oceanic whitetip may also be responsible for eating a consider amount of undocumented castaways. The oceanic whitetip are powerful and large predators, and they are known to attack and kill sometimes but their general nature can be inferred by the fact that all of the divers that have filmed them have been unprotected.

A French film in 2010 by the name of Oceans includes footage of sharks and humans swimming side by side out in the open ocean. Recent statistics document very few unprovoked attacks by whitetips.

In the exact opposite vein, Jacques Cousteau, who is infamous for his work as an oceanographic researcher, called them, "the most dangerous of all sharks." During both World War I and World War II, there were a number of attacks documented as well. Because of the world wars, there were many disasters involving aircrafts and ships, dropping the injured and bloody survivors into the whitetip's home.

The low death rate is at least partially due to the fact that these sharks do not leave the open ocean and have rarely every been seen around coastal areas, and the coasts are responsible for the most consistent documentation.

There are a few incidents involving oceanic whitetip shark attacks that are infamous in shark attack history. One of these was on November 18th of 1942 when the Nova Scotia, a steamship from Britain, sank after being hit with a German torpedo from a submarine.

They sank near South Africa and out of 1,000 passengers on board, only 192 survived. Many of the deaths were not just from the torpedo or the ship sinking, but from the oceanic whitetip shark as well. On July 20th of 1945, the USS Indianapolis was torpedoed as well and the whitetip are suspected to have been the cause of a considerable amount of the 60-80 deaths attributed to shark attacks.

It's plausible that the reason those divers are able to swim without fear of danger is that anything the oceanic whitetip would sense as food is covered by the unnatural elements that their diving gear is made of and the sharks will temporarily accept them as something new and worth curiosity instead of prey.

Surfers, snorkelers, and swimmers without diving gear are at a higher risk because of their exposed skin. The chances that a shark will attack heighten with the presence of even the smallest hint of blood in the water. Recent scabs and scrapes will make a person more likely to register as food.

The way that a shark finds its prey is through a biological ability called electroreception, which uses the electric fields that all animals naturally generate through the functional activity of muscles and nerves in order to sense their presence. It is also used as a communication device. This trait is almost completely exclusive to amphibious and aquatic animals, which is probably due to how much better water conducts than air. Currently, the known exceptions to this rule are echidnas, platypus, bees, and cockroaches.

The list of minor offenders on shark attacks is a little longer than the four already mentioned, and it includes the hammerhead, gray reef, shortfin mako, Galapagos, blacktip, silky shark, blue shark, and lemon sharks. The last new addition to the list of documented shark attack offenders was the cookiecutter shark on March 16th in 2009, when one attacked a long-distance swimmer that was making her hery through the Alenuihaha Channel that runs between Hawii' and Maui.

This incident was not vicious enough to be considered life-threatening, and though she was bitten twice the wounds were not severe. They are all powerful and large predators, and like any wild predator all it takes is being in the wrong place at the wrong time to provoke an attack. They are still considered much less aggressive with humans on average than the four previously mentioned.

The documented indexes that host the information on recorded shark attacks split them into two different main categories; provoked and unprovoked, though there are some that are not labeled as either. Examples include air and sea disaster casualties, which have their own category. Scavenging the remains of humans that are already dead is considered postmortem scavenging and is not considered provoked or unprovoked.

The Global Shark Attack File files postmortem biting as questionable incidents.

A provoked attack is brought upon a human after they touch a shark, tease it, poke it, spear it, hook it, net it, or aggravate it in any other way. In the wild, some of these provoked attacks are accidental, such as when a surfer bumps into a shark and gets bitten in response. All incidents that occur in captivity are classified as provoked, because capturing a shark is considered provocation, as is holding it outside of its natural habitat.

An unprovoked attack is one that the shark initiates, meaning the human involved did nothing to give the shark a reason to attack. In order to qualify as an unprovoked attack, the shark must also be in its natural habitat and the human must be alive. Within the main category that is unprovoked attacks, there are three subheadings:

- **Sneak attacks** are when the person that's attacked does not see the shark coming. These are strictly predatory attacks, which mean the intention is to kill and eat the victim, so the person may be bitten more than once... These types of attacks are very rare.

- **Hit-and-run attacks** are when the shark bites a person and then leaves. Most people that are bitten during hit-and-run attacks are only bitten once and do not see the shark. These types of attacks are the most common, and are generally not fatal. Most of these kinds of attacks happen in murky waters and surf zones and are suspected to be cases of sharks mistaking humans for other animals.

- **Bump-and-bite-attacks** are when the bite occurs after the shark circles the person and bumps them. Great white sharks are known to do this sometimes, and the bump is considered a test bite or a taste test, to find out what the person is before biting them. Because of this, mistaken identity has been taken off the list of possible causes for this type of attack. Panicking and thrashing after a bump-and-bite may result in the shark marking a person as prey, which will lead to multiple bites, though being bitten more than once is not uncommon in this kind of attack in general. These kinds of attacks can be severe, even fatal.

Unlike the common misconception might lead you to believe, most shark attacks are not about the shark wanting to eat a person for food. Sharks require a high calorie diet to provide them with enough energy to keep their large bodies running, and humans are just an inefficient food source for them. We don't have enough high-fat meat to be worth the effort it takes to eat us.

The most basic reasoning behind shark attacks is simple, especially for larger sharks; in their natural environment, they are apex predators. That means they have little to no fear of any other living being that they encounter, aside from orcas. They are also curious creatures, especially when they come across something in their territory that they find unusual or haven't seen around before, with their only efficient means of exploring an object being their mouth, and therefore their bite. Bites in the name of figuring out what something is are called test bites, and most of sharks that bite humans are just trying to figure out what the human is and they leave after their first bite.

A common example of these test bites are incidents involving surfers, in most cases of surf-related shark attacks, the sharks are thought to have mistaken the surfer and their board's shape to be the shape of beloved prey. However, even just one bite can severely injure or kill a person when the bite is coming from powerful predators like the tiger shark or great white shark.

With the subject of predators comes the subject of territory, which is another reason a shark might attack.

If the shark does decide that their victim is going to become their next meal, they will usually bite them once and then swim away to wait at a safe distance as their victim dies. This way, if their victim fights for their life, they won't be able to hurt the shark in the process. When it comes to human attacks, this running and waiting gives humans a chance to get out of the water and avoid become shark food.

Most documented examples of sharks attacking humans in a way that denotes they've targeted their victim as preys are just simple cases of mistaken identity. The Ampullae of Lorenzini are sensory organs that sharks use like electric radar that can detect the electricity in the water that muscle movement causes, which can mislead them. One example is mistaking human fishermen for the wounded fish they've been spearfishing, being led to the human by the electrical pulses emitted from the wounded fish.

Shark Attack Sprees

Between July 1st and July 12th of 1916, New Jersey was host to one of the most prolific series of shark attacks in shark attack history, known as the Jersey Shore shark attacks of 1916. This series of attacks by sharks were located in the United States, along the coastal line of New Jersey. Four human fatalities were documented as well as one injury. The species of shark that was responsible for these attacks has been up for debate since the year it happened has been debated between scholars, as well as the number of sharks that were involved in these attacks. The most commonly accused are the great white shark and the bull shark.

The background setting for these attacks was a polio epidemic with a deadly summer heat wave setting in the United States, inspiring thousands of people to pack up and head to New Jersey for a cool vacation at one of the many seaside resorts.

Between the dates of July 1st and 12ths in 1916, five people were involved in shark attacks off the coastal waters of New Jersey. July 1st was the first major attack, occurring on a Saturday at a resort town called Beach Haven, just off of Long Beach Island. The victim's name was Charles Epting Vansant, and he was 25 years old and on vacation from Philadelphia with his family. He decided that he wanted to head into the Atlantic Ocean for a little swim before dinner with a Chesapeake Bay Retriver he had been playing with on the beach. It wasn't long after he got in the water that Vansant was attacked. He started screaming, because the shark was biting his legs, but onlookers thought he was simply calling for the dog. There are claims that the shark followed them as far as it could up the shore as the bleeding man was pulled from the water by a lifeguard and a bystander. He survived the attack itself, but the skin on his left thigh was all gone and he bled to death in the Engleside Hotel, on the manager's desk.

Still, the beaches in the area remained open. One shark attack was not enough to cause enough panic or concern to cause beach activity to cease. Sea captains reported a number of larger sharks, but their documentation was dismissed. The resort

Town of Spring Lake, forty-five miles away from Beach Haven, was the site of the second attack. Charles Bruder was the victim, a 27 year old. It was July 6th, a Thursday when a shark bit him in the stomach and took his legs with it while he was swimming about 130 yards away from the beach's shore. There was enough blood in the water to turn it red. There were screams, which were reported along with the information that there was a capsized canoe floating in the water. A pair of lifeguards investigated the scene and surmised that a shark attack had occurred, and then pulled the victim out of the water. However, he died from blood loss before they made it back to the shore. Because of the severity of the mutilation to the victim's body, this death did spark panic.

The next two attacks in this spree were at the Matawan Creek, which is located near Keyport. The environment and location of this specific incident made it highly unlikely. It was Wednesday, the 12th of July, and a local sea captain had already sent in reports that stated that he'd seen a large shark in the creek, but his claims were dismissed by the town. At 2PM, some of the local boys were playing in an area called the Wyckoff dock and noticed there was something floating in the water. They thought it might be an old surfboard or a floating log when the dorsal fin of a shark emerged from the water and they realized that they were looking at a shark and exited the water. Lester Stilwell was 11 years old and the shark grabbed his whole body before he could get out of the creek and took him beneath the water. The second attack happened after the remaining boys ran to town for help and Watson Stanley Fisher, a local businessman at the age of 24, rushed into the water to investigate. He had just found Stilwell's body and was on his way out of the creek while the town watched the shark attack him as well, causing him to drop the boy. There was a severe injury located on his right thigh and he died of blood loss at the Monmouth Memorial Hospital. Stilwell's body wasn't seen again until July 14th.

The final victim was a 14 year old boy by the name of Joseph Dunn. His attack took place only half a mile away from the Wyckoff dock and only thirty minutes after Stilwell and Fisher were killed. The shark grabbed Dunn by the leg and a battle for his life was fought tug-of-war style between the shark and Dunn's friend. In the end, he was pulled away from the shark and taken to Saint Peter's University Hospital where he had a full recovery.

After these shark-related deaths, locals and citizens across the nation were sent into a panic by the first documented media coverage of a shark attack, inspiring shark hunts by those that wanted to rid the area of the violent, man-eating sharks they now feared. The media released caricatures of sharks as a representation of danger in editorial cartoons. It is said that the panic created by the media coverage of these serial shark attacks was previously unrivaled in American history, and it covered the coastal areas from New Jersey and New York, spreading further with every letter, phone call, and postcard.

Resort towns had their beaches enclosed with steel shark barriers to keep their seaside resort economy afloat. At that point in history, most of the official scientific knowledge in relation to sharks was based on pure speculation and conjecture, and these attacks ichthyologists to question some of their beliefs in regards to the behaviors and power of sharks and the facts behind shark attacks. These attacks were also later researched and documentaries have used them as their subject, including documentaries for the National Geographic Channel, the History Channel, and the Discovery Channel.

Black December is the name of a series of nine separate shark attacks against humans along the KwaZulu-Natal coast in South Africa that killed six of the victims. These attacks took place between December 18th of 1957 and April 5th of 1958. It is said that the perfect storm of factors combined and attracted sharks to the Durban area. Some of these factors included the rivers flooding and washing livestock animals into the Indian Ocean, the river deltas being murky, the operation of whaling ships in the area, and the recent increase in developments for resorts that brought more tourists into the waters at their beaches. Not having enough research on sharks to give the public the information they needed to soothe their fears led to confusion, and of course, more fear.

The victims of Black December include Fay Jones Bester who was 28 at the time and died from a fatal attack while she was surfing. Nicholaas Badenhorst was 29 when he died from a fatal attack that included a bite to the abdomen and leg as well as a bite that took his arm off completely right above the elbow while he was swimming. Derryck Garth Prinsloo died at the age of 42 from a fatal attack that severed his femoral artery by destroying his body from the waist down while he was standing in the water. An unknown man in Zulu was also killed in 1958 at an unknown age when his right leg was removed right above the knee while he was out fishing. Vernon James Berry was 23 when he died of a fatal shark attack that broke his right arm and stripped the skin off of it, severed his left hand, and left his buttocks, thigh, and lower abdomen bitten while he was floating in the water. Allan Green was 15 when he suffered while he was standing in the water an attack that took his life, leaving him with severe injuries. Julia Painting, who was 14 at the time, suffered an attack while standing in the water that wasn't fatal, leaving her alive but with her left arm removed, a bite to the torso, thigh lacerations, and many other cuts and abrasions. Donald Webster was another victim of an attack that wasn't fatal, and he suffered lacerations on his head and neck while he was skin diving. Robert Werley was 16 when he suffered a non-fatal shark attack that severed his left leg at the knee and took part of his left thigh while he was surfing.

After the attacks of Black December, 1962 hosted the formation of the Natal Sharks Board (which was also known as the Natal Anti-Shark Measures Board and then later the DwaZulu-Natal Sharks Board). The purpose of the organization was to protect surfers and swimmers by maintaining drum lines and shark nets at a total of thirty-eight different locations, covering 320 km of coastal area along South African KwaZulu-Natal Province.

In 2010, there were a series of shark attacks against people swimming in the Egypt resort of Sharm El Sheikh off the Red Sea. This series of attacks was called the 2010 Sharm El Sheikh Shark attacks. The first attacks in this series occurred on the 1st of December and included three Russians and one Ukrainian victim that were attacked and injured severely within a span of just a few minutes. The 5th of December hosted the second part of this spree of shark attacks, when a German woman was attacked while wading near the shoreline and was killed. Experts that have studied the area and this event call it unprecedented. As of December of 2010, the theory with the most plausibility is that people were dumping the bodies of sheep that died in livestock transportation into the Red Sea, which attracted the sharks closer to the shore. Other theories blame overfishing, which would overload the area with electronic signals that told sharks there were injured fish in the water. Still more theories focus on inadvertent and illegal shark feeding near the shore, or the feeding of smaller fish that attracted more sharks. For over a full week after the attacks, all of the beaches in the area were closed down. The response from citizens in the area was to launch a shark hunt that ended in dozens of sharks being captured and then killed, while the government released new laws that banned the act of feeding sharks and restricted the areas and times people could swim.

The Great White Shark

The Great White Shark is not only arguably one of the most recognizable and well known shark species, but it is also one of the most dangerous as one marine mammal's primary predatory species. This species' scientific name is Carcharodon carcharias and it is also known by the names white pointer, great white, white death, and white shark. It is a large mackerel species of shark and has been spotted in the surface waters off the coasts of all of the major oceans. The only known natural predator of the great white shark is the killer whale.

A great deal of the fear surrounded the great white shark come from the movie Jaws, which features a large and purposefully aggressive shark that seems to enjoy nothing more than hunting and killing humans. There have been many other movies that feature at least one man-eating, bloodthirsty great white sharks since then as well. In fact, sharks are one of the more common villains featured in horror movies, whether they're genetically or supernaturally modified or just plain aggressive naturally.

The power behind the bite of a great white shark that is approximately 7,328 pounds is equal to 18,216 newtons. Younger great white sharks have jaws that are less developed and therefore weaker, lowering the strength of their bite and forcing them to stick with fish as their prey because they are physically incapable of the jaw power required to go after bigger prey. After they've reached a length of at least three meters (or 9.8 feet) the cartilage in their jaw mineralizes to the point that they can bite and chew larger prey without injuring their jaw. One newton is the equivalent of the force of one apple. The average force of the Earth's gravity is about 9.8 newtons. The force of an action is measured by newtons, as the International System of Units for force. The name is in recognition to Isaac Newton, specifically in reference and reverence to his second law of motion.

The reasoning behind why great white sharks attack humans, how their hunting patterns and behaviors are determined, and how they respond in a shark attack situation is dependent on a variety of different information.

When it comes to food, the great white are known for eating other marine life, which include fish as well as seabirds. In the genus Carcharodon, it is the only species to have survived. The favorite meal of a great white shark is not humans, but when it comes to shark attacks, its ranked number one for being responsible for more fatal, documented shark attacks against humans than any other shark species. Despite, or perhaps because of human response to that fact, it is on the IUCN as a listed, vulnerable species.

The diet of a great white shark is, not surprisingly, strictly carnivorous. Their prey includes fish like rays, tuna, and other sharks, as well as cetaceans like porpoises, dolphins, and whales, pinnipeds like fur seals, seals, and sea lions, and sea otters, sea lions, and sea birds. After surpassing four meters (or 13 feet), it is common for great white sharks to move on from a diet consistent of fish and begin targeting more marine mammals than fish. There is an obvious preference in individual great white sharks as well, giving some of them different eating habits depending on what their favorite tastes are. Great white sharks have also been known to eat things that are not food that their bodies cannot digest, which are found inside the stomachs of dead great whites, partially or completely undigested. They're opportunistic creatures that turn to prey with high levels of fat, because that kind of prey will give them a more substantial amount of energy.

One such common prey of great white sharks off the coasts of California is northern elephant seals. The sharks will immobilize the animal with one powerful hit-and-run bite, leaving the injury to lead to death by blood loss before they return to claim their meal. Most northern elephant seals are bigger than the great whites that are hunting them, on average, so the bite-and-run tactic allows the shark to remain safe from any fight the elephant seal might want to give to try and save its life. The most common method for picking off elephant seals is by picking stragglers off at the edges of colonies though. In these instances, the great white shark will grab an elephant seal from somewhere close to the surface of the water, bite it so that it can hold it tightly, and then drag it down below the surface until it stops struggling. The actual process of eating the elephant seal happens as close to the bottom of the sea bed as is conveniently possible.

Surfers are often attacked because a shark has mistaken them for some form of seal.

There is not very much that is understood about the social structure and behavior of the great white shark and it seems to differ from location to location. There is a dominance hierarchy in South Africa between great white sharks that is dependent upon the sex, size, and territory rights. Females reign over the males, with larger sharks dominating those that are smaller than it, and long-time residents of specific territories having more control than newcomer sharks. Separation and physical displays are the most common form of problem solving in the great white shark communities, with physical aggression and violence being rather low on their list of usual resources. There have been incidents of great white sharks being spotted with marks on them that appear to have been left behind by other great whites though, which suggests that there is a limit to their general passive stance towards each other. These marks are thought to be warning bites, meant to tell a great white shark they're getting too close to their fellow great white shark. These bites could also be a simple show of dominance.

Unlike most other sharks, the great white's swimming patterns include breaching the surface of the water like a whale or a dolphin. It is theorized that this action is taken in order to look or smell things better, including prey. Smells travel better through air than they do water. It is also theorized that this is a learned behavior that was picked up after watching humans in the case of at least one group of blacktip reef sharks.

They don't often travel alone either, an example of which is the sightings of groupings of two to six great white sharks traveling together at Seal Island. It isn't known whether or not the individual sharks within these traveling groups are related to each other or not. They appear to function in a similar fashion to the way a pack of wolves operates, with each individual shark being given specific tasks that keep the group alive along with a rank, with one shark being the alpha leader. Travel is one of the different reasons that great white sharks turn to socializing, and they show signs of intelligence and curiosity.

Two out of three of the most infamous and biggest serial shark attacks were potentially perpetrated by great white sharks. The Jersey Shore incidents in 1916 were probably committed at the teeth of a great white shark, and are arguably the title holder for most infamous shark attacks in history. Four people were killed and one was injured over the span of ten days. These serial shark attacks were the first media publicized shark attacks and are believed to be the inspiration behind the making of Jaws. It is also possible that this series of shark attacks was committed by a bull shark. It is also speculated that a great white shark is responsible for the attack that occurred a week later on a young boy and the citizen that jumped into the Matawan Creek in search of his body.

Another infamous attack perpetrated by a great white shark was against Rodney Fox in 1953. He was defending his title as a champion in Australian spearfishing when he was taken into the jaws of a great white shark by the waist. The severity of his injuries has earned him the title of most well-known survivor of a shark attack; the fact that he survived has been called miraculous.

Another possible inspiration for the movie Jaws was the attack on Barry Wilson in 1952. During this attack, a seventeen year old boy was killed violently in front of a large crowd of witnesses. It was reported that the visuals on the attack began with a swift jerk to one side before he was pulled from one side to another. He was then dragged out of the water completely before being pulled back down and dragged under completely.

Lloyd Skinner was the victim of a shark attack perpetrated by a shark that is believed to be a great white based on witness reports. It is said that Lloyd Skinner was swimming in waters that reached his neck, wading just a few yards away from the beach's shore in a place in South Africa called Cape Town. The attack was so quick that it was over in just a few seconds, with Lloyd being pulled under water and then disappearing without a trace. The only sign that he had even been there was a pool of blood and the goggles he'd worn to swim.

Another infamous attack perpetrated by great white sharks was in 1964 and is the first shark attack to be captured via film. A man by the name of Henri Bource was in the company of two other fellow divers and took a swim in Australia, off the coast. A great white shark appeared and went immediately for Henri, taking one of his legs in its mouth. He was saved by his colleagues, who were able to pull him to safety and then administer first aid. When interviewed on the subject of his attack, Henri claimed to have tried to gouge the shark's eyes out and choke it by shoving his arm down its throat in an attempt to get free.

The Tiger Shark

The species genus name for the tiger shark is Galeocerdo Cuvier, and they are a variety of shark known as requiem sharks. They are more commonly referred to as the sea tiger, and can be as big as more than sixteen feet and five inches long. They have dark stripes along their body, hence the name. They frequent the central Pacific islands, more specifically waters that are temperate or tropical.

Unlike the great white shark, most tiger sharks are completely solitary. They are also more prone to hunting at night, and it should be noted that their standard diet includes the widest variety in all species of sharks. They've been known to feed on fish, crustaceans, birds, seals, turtles, squid, and even sharks that are smaller than they are. Like the great white, they're also known for ingesting man-made objects that cannot be digested and are later found in autopsies. Because of the amount of inedible objects found in the bellies of tiger sharks, they're also sometimes called garbage eaters. Because it has a spot on the list of three most common shark attack offenders, it is also often called the man-eater shark in a colloquial sense. Their only concern as far as fellow predators in their natural habitats are concerned, are the threat posed by killer whales, or orcas, which are known to attack and feed on sharks. Unfortunately, humans make the list of threats to the tiger shark population as well. The practice of fishing for tiger sharks or finning them has pushed their population numbers so low that they are near consideration as a threatened species.

The tiger shark is mostly nomadic, which means that they frequently move from place to place, with the temperature of the water being a major factor in where they decide to go. The warmer the water, the more likely they will be to follow its currents. Because of this, they tend to stay close to the equator, especially during the cold months of the winter season. They also have a preference for deep water, but they are known to travel to shallower depths in the name of chasing food.

The teeth on a tiger shark are unique in their shapes, with their pronounced and very sharp serrations. Another unique attribute to the teeth of a tiger shark are the way the sideways pointing tip that is unmistakable. These features allow the tiger shark to use their teeth to bite through tough materials, like turtle shells, flesh, and bone. Just like most species of sharks, the tiger shark's teeth are also replaced in an infinite cycle throughout the span of their life. Compared to the size of the great white shark's teeth in comparison to their body size, it can be argued that the size of a tiger shark's teeth in comparison to their body size makes them more effectively crafted for the task of slicing through prey with thick skin or tough surfaces.

As one can imagine, tiger sharks are considered apex predators and have earned themselves a reputation as an animal that will eat anything. Great white sharks are known for being found with license plates and other human paraphernalia in their stomachs, but they are still not regarded as the same level of trash-eater as the tiger shark.

The hunting behaviors among tiger sharks show that they have a preference for swimming closer to the coasts at night to feed on prey and spend much of their day out in deeper waters, occupied with swimming, The fact that they come close to the shore to hunt for prey, visiting places like canals, shallow reefs, and harbors, puts them in places where human interaction is more likely. Younger tiger sharks have a diet that consists mostly of small fish, small jellyfish, cephalopods, and other types of mollusks. They near their sexual maturity by the time they're around 7.5 feet in length and their diet expands greatly. At that size, they can hunt and eat much bigger prey, making numerous larger fish, sea birds, sea snakes, marine mammals, crustaceans, bottlenose dolphins, spotted dolphins, common dolphins, rays, sea turtles, seals, sea lions, and dugongs a regular part of the menu as well. 20.8% of tiger sharks that have had their stomach contents studied had turtle in their stomachs, proving that turtles are a consistent part of the general diet of tiger sharks, either because there is a consistent supply of them that cross their path naturally or they actively hunt turtles as a preference. Tiger sharks are also known to feed on other sharks, even other tiger sharks.

Tiger sharks are so often responsible for attacks against dolphins that as a general rule, if there are tiger sharks; dolphins will avoid the whole region. They've been documented as being responsible for attacking whales that are injured or sick as well as feeding on those that are already dead. One such documented attack on was near Hawaii in 2006, when a group of tiger sharks killed a sick humpback whale. In the case of scavenging on dead whales, they've been seen feeding beside great white sharks as well.

Tiger sharks have excellent vision, a highly developed sense of smell, and serrated, strong teeth that allow them to follow blood trails and then opportunistically attack the already injured victim at the end of the trail.

The fact that they can read electric impulses in the water and low-frequency pressure waves gives the tiger shark a reason to be confidence when it chooses to attack, even if the water is cloudy and difficult to see through the use of just its eyes. The tiger shark is known to circle its intended victim and then poke at it with the tip of its face. During an attack, tiger sharks are known to swallow their food whole. This may be done in order to quickly ingest their prey before they can fight back and injure the shark on the way down. In the case of larger prey, they do often have to eat more gradually, finishing their food over time in multiple bites.

Infamous shark attacks on humans that are attributed to tiger sharks include the attack on Bethany Hamilton in 2003. At the age of thirteen, Bethany was ranked as one of America's top surfers when she was attacked by a tiger shark in Hawaii and lost her arm. The shark attack did not take her interest in surfing away, or birth enough fear in her to stop her from surfing. She has since won the 2005 national surfing title.

On average, there are a total of three or four reported shark bites in Hawaii every year, with very few of those cases being fatal. These biting incidents are attributed to tiger sharks, and are considered low in comparison to the high thousands of people that surf, dive, and swim in the waters of Hawaii every day. The amount of documented human interaction with tiger sharks in the area is known to rise between the months of September and November, which is believed to be attributed to females migrating to give birth near the islands.

Another notable fact in tiger shark history refers to the culling of 4,668 tiger sharks from 1959 to 2000. These efforts have severely damaged the population of tiger sharks, which are now near endangered, and proved to be wholly ineffective in their efforts to reduce the amount of shark attacks caused by tiger sharks and interactions between tiger sharks and humans in general have not gone down either. Any and all interaction with tiger sharks is discouraged in Hawaii, and feeding them is illegal, except in the instance of certain religious practices and Hawaiian cultural traditions.

Despite the obvious reasons that there are people who fear tiger sharks, there have been documented instances of friendly interactions between them and humans. Specific instances include a Discover Channel special that was filmed in 2007, featuring a shark diver and behaviorist from South Africa by the name of Mark Addison proving that safe interaction between a diver and a tiger shark is possible without the use of a shark cage. Further well known examples of successfully friendly interaction between tiger sharks and humans was seen when Fiona Ayerst, a photographer that specializes in underwater photography, took the time to go swimming with tiger sharks in the Bahamas. The practice of diving without the use of cages to interact with female tiger sharks has even become a consistently routine practice in a place off the Grand Bahama known as Tiger Beach.

The Bull Shark

The final of the three most common perpetrators of shark attacks against humans are the bull sharks. The scientific name for the bull shark is Carcharhunus leucas, and they are also called the Zambezi shark or Zambezi River shark in Africa; with the unofficial, colloquial name for them being Zambi or Nicaragua shark in Nicaragua. Among some of the other names that the bull shark has earned, Fitzroy Creek whaler, Ganges River shark, Lake Nicaragua shark, river shark, estuary whaler, freshwater whaler, Swan River whaler, shovelnose shark, cub shark, and van Rooyen's shark are amount them. Some of these names were given to the bull shark based on locations they are known to frequent, and there are a lot of different types of habitats that they are known to frequent. It is classified as a requiem shark and is most often found along coastal waters and rivers in the warm, shallow waters all over the world.

Before 1961, the bull sharks in Lake Nicaragua were thought to be an entirely different and new species of shark. They were called the Lake Nicaragua shark, of the genus Carcharhinus nicaraguensis, but specimens were later compared by scientists and researchers that proved they were the same species, so taxonomists dubbed both names for the shark as synonymous.

Bull sharks are known to be aggressive by nature, and are capable of surviving both fresh and salt water conditions, which allows them to travel through rivers, making it great distances away from the ocean. In fact, they're infamously known for making trips up the Mississippi River. On some of these trips, some bull sharks have crossed so much distance on the Mississippi that they end up in Illinois. Luckily, there are still very few interactions between humans and bull sharks that take place in fresh water. Many of the attacks that take place close in or around coastal waters are probably perpetrated by bull sharks, even some of the attacks that have been pinned on other shark species.

Though they can survive in fresh water, bull sharks are not truly freshwater sharks. They are born in the ocean and the majority of them spend most of their lives in ocean waters. Still, they are one of only forty-three total species in the elasmobranch category that have been reportedly sighted in water without salt. The classification name for their ability to survive easily in both types of water is diadromous. The ability to adapt to various levels of saline also classifies them as a euryhaline fish. Very few fish that have cartilage are able to survive in freshwater. Most of the other fish that fit in this category have bones, like tilapia and the salmon. These other euryhaline fish are not at all related to bull sharks historically, and how bull sharks ended up qualifying for the category is up for debate. Many scientists believe that their population hit a point where it bottlenecked, plausibly sometime during the last ice age. Because of this bottleneck in population, the bull shark had to evolve in a way that pushed them away in this biological sense from all other creatures in the subclass that is Elasmobranchii by taking hold of the genes that are responsible for the osmoregulatory system.

If a bull shark wanted to, it could spend its entire life living in fresh water. One of the main reasons this does not happen very often is reproduction. Breeding generally happens in the open ocean for bull sharks, so even if they are born in fresh water, they are inclined to journey until they find the salt water of the ocean so that they can mate and reproduce. It is theoretically possible for a bull shark to survive for the span of its entire life within fresh water, though it should also be noted that there was an experiment around the subject that ended in all of the test subjects dying within just four short years. These sharks were not kept in captivity, but were kept in fresh water. Upon their deaths, they were autopsied and the stomach contents gave the scientists just a few fish to study. It is very likely that bull sharks are more likely to live shorter lives in fresh water because their main sources of food are all found in salt water, so they die from starvation outside of it.

Another fact that was observed during studies like this is that the younger a bull shark is, the more likely it is that it will be found in fresh water. Newborn bull sharks have a very low tolerance for the change from freshwater to salt water. The ability to tolerate salinity comes with age and physical maturity, so the bull sharks found out in the ocean are usually adults.

Bull sharks were given their name for their unpredictable and aggressive behavior, as well as for the shape of their body and their snout. As far as physical appearance is concerned, they are also generally known to be heavier and wider than the other sharks under the requiem classification and their general size makes them comparable by length as well.

The bite force of a bull shark can be up to 5,914 newtons strong, which is the highest number earned by any of the cartilaginous fish that have been investigated based on weight for weight.

Bull sharks are physically strong enough that like salmon, they can actually jump up raving rapids against the powerful flow of water. An example is bull sharks climbing the San Juan River rapids and fighting their way to Lake Nicaragua from the Caribbean Sea. There are bull sharks that were tagged in the lake that made the journey back to the open ocean, just like there have been bull sharks tagged in the ocean that made their way up to the lake. In some instances, the whole trip took as little as seven to ten days from start to finish.

As previously stated, bull sharks prefer to reside in warmer coastal areas, in lakes and rivers, and can also be found in both freshwater and saltwater streams from time to time if they're deep enough. They can be found in water that is up to 490 feet deep and they are not usually found any deeper than ninety-eight feet. They can also survive waters as salty as the St. Lucia Estuary in South African as well as water completely free of salt. They are found from southern Brazil all the way to Massachusetts in the Atlantic Ocean and then from Angola to Morroco. In the Indian Ocean, they have been spotted from Australia to South Africa to India, Kenya, Philippines, and Vietnam. The Pacific Ocean hosts them from Ecuador to Baja California. Historically, the bull shark is responsible for making a 2,500 mile trip to north Bolivia and Iquitos in Peru through the Amazon River. In the United States, they have made it as far up the Ohio River as the location Manchester in Ohio. Another United States located place they've been seen is called the Potomac River and it is located in Maryland. There are also high populations of bull sharks in many different major rivers. One such river is the Brisbane River, and it is believed that there are a total of more than 500 bull sharks living there.

They have been spotted during natural disasters; one such example saw reports of a bull shark swimming the streets after Brisbane was flooded during the Queensland floods of 2010 to 2011. There have been other examples of bull sharks reportedly swimming through flooded city streets, including an incident reported after the floods in January of 2011 peaked in Goodna, Queensland where multiple bull sharks were said to be seen on one of their main city streets. Hurricane Katrina brought many of the bull sharks in the area to Lake Pontchartrain, where they were later sighted.

Most of a bull shark's diet is made up on small sharks and bony fish. They're even known for eating other bull sharks. Other items on the bull shark menu include birds, turtles, terrestrial mammals, dolphins, echinoderms, stingrays, and crustaceans. Their usual hunting grounds are murky, making it different for the creatures it sees as prey to see it coming while the shark itself can rely on other senses to make up for the lack in visibility. They prefer to use a technique against their prey that involves bumping into them, biting them, and then running away to let them die with enough distance between the shark and its prey to stop it from getting hurt by the desperate attempts of a dying animal. If necessary, they will continue to repeat the bite-and-run technique multiple times, tackling their prey and biting them until they are incapable of fleeing before the shark swims back to give them space to flail and fight the open water until they succumb to their injuries.

Though some of the creatures they feed on and hunt as prey are rather big and formidable, bull sharks still show a preference towards solitary hunting. There are exceptions, where bull sharks have teamed up against other bull sharks and bigger prey in order to make the task easier for all of the sharks that will get to eat after the kill.

As that behavior is evidence of, bull sharks are like all sharks in the sense that they are known to be incredibly opportunistic when it comes to their feeding habits, much like vultures and other animals that take down a decent amount of their prey through luck and circumstance instead of relying solely on the power of their sheer, brute force. The normal eating habits of sharks include eating as much as possible in short bursts, pigging out at various points. During times when it's harder to find food and weaker prey is scarce, sharks are capable of slowing down their metabolism a great deal in order to spend more time digesting, which lowers the chances of them starving to death.

Bull sharks are also known to throw up any food that they have in their stomach if they feel they are being threatened by a predator, and this survival mechanism allows them to escape while their predator is distracted; the moment that the larger predator makes a move to dine on the bull shark's last meal, the bull shark itself runs, avoiding the larger predator's attempts to eat it as a meal instead.

In general, bull sharks do not tolerate provocation and have nearly no tolerance at all for anything that they don't like, especially if they feel threatened by it. That mixed with their love for the many different types of habitats that are located in the warm, shallow waters near the coasts of the world are the recipe that make them one of the most dangerous species of shark to humans.

One infamous example of bull sharks mixing ineffectively with humans was recorded in the Sydney Harbor inlets, and involved bull sharks biting swimmers. Many of these attacks were originally thought to be caused by great white sharks, but were later found to be caused by bull sharks.

Shark Attack Prevention

As a cause of death worthy of its own statistics, shark attacks also have a variety of different techniques that can be used to reduce the risks so that people are safer. These techniques include keeping people separate from sharks, taking sharks away when people intrude through different methods used in fishing, as well as observing sharks to learn more, educating people on the subject of sharks, and a variety of different solutions based in technology.

On top of technology, nature has provided humans with protection in the form of dolphins. Instances where bottlenose dolphins protected humans from attacking sharks have been documented. One such instance took place in New Zealand, off the coast in 2004. Another attack was interrupted in 2007 when a dolphin saved a surfer in norther California. Although much is known about the behavior of most animals that we share the planet with, there is no official explanation behind this behavior. There have not been enough studies done to give substantial evidence to prove or create any theories, though there have been many who question it and speculate. There are documented reports of sharks attacking dolphins in the wild, but just because one is around, does not mean the other is absent. It isn't guaranteed that having a dolphin around will stop a shark attack though, and it is also not a guarantee that one will step in to fight for the human being attacked. There are documented reports of sharks attacking surfers while dolphins were present.

There are extremists that have brought the term culling into being, which is a government implemented capturing and then killing of sharks to reduce their population numbers. One such example of a shark cull took place in Western Australia, which has already been stated as one of the most dangerous places in the world for shark attacks. It started in December of 2014 and lasted until March of 2017, and the shark cull allowed the Australian government to explore areas that had a high shark attack rate so that they could kill any shark they deemed dangerous to humans. Many are opposed to the idea, both when it was implemented in Australia and in general, just as many are opposed to all types of harming animals. Scientists and environmentalists have said for a long time that population numbers for all species are linked, and there is no way of knowing what the removal of sharks could be doing to the rest of the ecosystem they are being taken out of.

A common technique for preventing shark attacks is the use of a shark net. Most shark nets use what are called gillnets, which is a netting wall much like what most people imagine a fishing net looks like. These are set to hang in the open water, positioned to capture sharks by tangling them in it, and once the shark is tangled, it will die. Some of these gillnets are up to 610 feet in length with and go down twenty feet deep. Nets of that size are designed with the intention of ensnaring sharks that are longer than 6.6 feet from nose to tail.

There are problems associated with shark nets, which include catching and killing species that they weren't intended to kill, which can include endangered and harmless species. Their efficiency is due completely to the fact that killing sharks' means there are fewer sharks, and less sharks means the chances of any of them attacking is lower because there are less of them to factor in. Technically, the use of shark nets suggests that it might reduce the number of shark attacks when they are used consistently.

In New South Wales, their shark netting program costed them an approximated $1 million. This money funded the contractors, bought the nets, bought the shark meshing equipment, paid the observers and shark technicians, and paid for the compliance audit activities. There are fifty-one beaches in total that are protected under this program, which is an approximated $20,000 per year, per beach.

Another common form of shark attack prevention is known as shark barriers, beach enclosures, and shark-proof enclosures. All three terms describe the same technique, which is a netted barrier that is placed that goes from the surface of the water all the way down to the seabed that wraps around a beach to keep any wandering sharks away from the beach. These shark barriers enclose the entire span of the area that people can swim, completely blocking the entry of sharks. The first shark barriers were made of the most basic fencing materials, but have since evolved into more suitable plastics and netting materials with anchors and buoys.

These are considered to be the better and more environmentally friendly option for shark attack prevention, because the purpose is to deter sharks from swimming too close to shore, not to kill them. There is also much less danger of bycatch, so other species aren't put in danger by this method. However, beaches that are popular with surfers can't successfully make use of shark barriers because the swell is strong enough to break them. Unfortunately, surfers are also one of the more common targets, because the way they swim before catching a wave makes them look like one of shark's favorite prey. For that reason, they are usually only used on harbor beaches and other areas that are sheltered, leaving the water smooth and gentle.

A shark barrier can be expensive, because of how long they run. For instance, the installation of the shark barrier at Middleton beach in Albany, Western Australia was $340,000 and the budget covers $30,000 worth of maintenance annually.

Another form of shark attack prevention is called a drum line, which is an aquatic trap that runs unmanned with the use of a lure and baited hooks to catch large sharks. They are most commonly used near beaches where swimming is popular, with the hope of lowering the probability of shark attacks by lowering the population of the sharks in the area. Both shark nets and shark barriers are used to complete the same purpose, but drum lines target the three sharks that are responsible for the majority of shark attacks more effectively. However, they have been defamed because they are destructive to the environment and have been criticized for being speciesist. A combination of both vocal opposition and public demonstrations has been held against the use of drum lines, especially from animal welfare advocates, ocean activists, and environmentalists.

The first time these were used was in 1962 in Queensland, Australia, and they were just as effective as shark nets when it came to reducing the number of shark attacks. A more recent example of the use of drum lines was in Recife, Brazil. After the drum lines were installed and deployed, there was a 97% reduction in shark attacks.

The price of a three-month long trial period with sixty drums set up in Western Australia cost a total of $1.28 million.

Other protection methods are more environmentally safe and don't include the need to kill sharks in order to lower the risk of attack.

One of these shark attack prevention techniques is called shark spotting, but it's not very effective. It requires paying people for surveillance work and/or hiring aircraft personnel. Shark spotting uses helicopters, drones, beach patrols, fixed wing aircraft towers, blimps, and observation towers to watch sharks so that attacks can be avoided by revealing their locations. However, it's not always easy to see through the water, or see very deep, so less than 20% of the sharks in the area can actually be seen through this technique, which makes the financial tax of hiring all of those people less worth the cost.

Shark tagging and tracking is more efficient for collecting the same information. A collection of sharks around the world have been safely tagged with devices that emit electronic pulses that give their locations to the groups in charge of these studies. Another common method of tagging sharks is via a satellite mounted on their fins. Underwater listening stations pick up these electric pulses at approximately 600 meters, which are transmitted by acoustic tags. Through this technique, the movements of these sharks can be tracked and recorded, allowing environmentalists the use of that valuable information when working on further actions to take in shark attack prevention.

However, it isn't possible to tag every single shark out in the ocean. In fact, only a very low percentage of dangerous sharks are tagged, which can give a false sense of safety to those that forget about the undocumented shark population.

Another method of shark attack prevention is called the Shark Shield. A Shark Shield makes shark attacks less likely by creating a personal electromagnetic field that encircles the user to stop sharks from wanting to approach them. It's popular among surfers, spearfishes, scuba divers, and ocean kayakers that fish. As far as shark attack prevention tools that an independent consumer can purchase are concerned, it's the only one to be verified independently as effective in its purpose.

In government, is has been announced that the West Australian government supports the Shark Shield model FREEDOM 7 and has given them a $200 subsidiary. As of April 2017, the diver version of the Shark Shield is the only one to have been officially approved and given that rebate.

However, this shark attack prevention technique doesn't work in every situation. There have been reported incidents of divers that are still attacked while using a Shark Shield.

Other means of shark attack prevention that can be used by the individual consumer are shark repellents. Things that can be used to repel sharks include semiochemicals, electropositive shark repellents, magnetic shark repellents, and electrical repellents; of which the Shark Shield qualifies as. One of the more popular shark repellents is an extract from the tissue of a dead shark that is put in an aerosol can and called the Anti-Shark 100. A variety of different sources of evidence have proved the product to be effective.

Other things that an average person can do to prevent shark attacks include wearing camouflage or patterned wetsuits, acoustic repellents that keep sharks away by sounding like orcas, magnetic repellents that come in the shape of a wrist or ankle band with a small magnet in it, and specific colors for surf boards. None of the techniques listed in this paragraph have been officially proven through testing though.

Shark Attack Prevention by Country

Shark prevention initiatives vary from country to country, with each one having its own preferences and laws in regards to the protection of the environment and the treatment of animals.

As one of the leaders in shark attack frequency, the United States has quite a bit of history with shark attack prevention. In Hawaii alone, between the years of 1959 and 1976 there were seven shark culls that ran short term and used long-lines. A total of 4,668 sharks were caught during these culls, which cost the United States $300,000. Because of this, the number of tourists raised dramatically, while the shark attack numbers were consistent with previous years, despite the increase in human population. Shark culling study authors have dubbed these short term culls ineffective and unsuccessful, because there did not seem to be any effect on the number of Hawaiian water local shark attacks. At the time, there was also intense debating about the culling in Hawaii. This debate was sparked by the death of Martha Morrel by shark attack in November of 1991, off the coast of Maui. This death also inspired the formation of the Hawaii Shark Task Force.

Because Western Australia is known as one of the deadliest places in terms of shark attacks, it also has a deep history in shark attack prevention. In total, there were 111 unprovoked attacks by sharks between the years of 1870 and 2016, with ten recorded shark-related deaths since 2010. Drum lines are deployed by the Western Australian government in the case of certain, specific circumstances. The policy that allows this is known as the imminent threat policy, and allows the government to search out and kill any shark or sharks it deems a potential threat to humans. There are also many different beach locations in Western Australia that are protected by beach enclosures that stop sharks from swimming too close to where people swim by the shore through the use of netted fencing. They also use a variety of different shark spotting techniques, as well as shark tagging and beach patrols in order to study the behaviors of the nearby shark population in order to better predict what measures in shark attack prevention will be the best fit.

South Australia is less notoriously dangerous based on statistics and has less in the name of shark prevention programs. They patrol a small number of their swimming beaches and use spotter planes to watch the behavior of the local shark population. These two things are the only government-run programs to prevent shark attacks. As of September of 2014, there were eighty-two officially reported instances of sharks attacking in South Australia, since the year 1836, with twenty of those leading to fatalities. A successful tuna farmer that operated spotter planes for his business to watch shark behavior stated that he had seen more great white sharks populating the Eyre

Peninsula, off of the west coast. The business of tuna farming attracts sharks, as tuna is a major source of food for them.

Systematic, long term programs for shark control have been implemented in Queensland and New South Wales that combine the usage of drum lines and shark nets to lower the statistical probability of shark attacks. Shark nets have been used on beaches in Sydney since 1936, and they're used on beaches in New South Wales now as well. There are a total of eighty-three beaches with shark nets and fifty-one in New South Wales.

Shark Attacks in the Media: News and Fiction

More than any actual, real events involving shark attacks, the fear of shark attacks is often based on fictional concepts. Media has successfully impacted the public's general view of sharks and shark attacks in a negative way, causing more unfounded panic than good. When news of a shark attack is broadcast, especially if the attack led to any fatalities, a general sense of shark panic arises.

This shark panic is generally inspired by fiction, and fears associated and inspired by it. One of the most iconic and well known movies of all time is Jaws, a movie about a rabidly killer shark. After its initial release, shark phobia rose exponentially and thousands of sharks are said to have died in response to that fear. In order to try and counter-balance the negative coverage on sharks and shark attacks, programs like Shark Week serve to educate the public by giving them truths that will ease that shark fear.

There is fear based on reality as well. Four people were killed in 1916 just the first two weeks of July in what is known as the Jersey Shore shark attacks. These attacks took place along the Matawan Creek and New Jersey shore, and are generally acknowledged as the first United States news media coverage of shark attacks.

Nine Australians that have survived shark attacks came together in 2010 in order to support sharks in a more positive way. These survivors called the media out for their negative slanting against sharks, and how their words could distort the public's view and cause a fear of sharks.

Printed in Great Britain
by Amazon